ENTANGLED

poems by

EMILY CHURCH

Finishing Line Press
Georgetown, Kentucky

ENTANGLED

*for my children
and my parents*

Copyright © 2024 by Emily Church
ISBN 979-8-88838-447-3 First Edition
All rights reserved under International and Pan-American Copyright Conventions. No part of this book may be reproduced in any manner whatsoever without written permission from the publisher, except in the case of brief quotations embodied in critical articles and reviews.

ACKNOWLEDGMENTS

I want to thank Derek, Ursula, and Orion Gluckman, and Dan and Janie Church for endless support, encouragement, and inspiration. And thank you to the following people for your close reading, comments, technical and emotional support: Lisa Andrews, Merle Bachman, Peter Mallo, Kate Milford, Delany Schucker, Amy Seibert, Sarah Yost, and Halley Zien. Thank you to the editors of Finishing Line Press for the opportunity to bring this chapbook to fruition.

"Summer of Bees," "Gingko," "On the Eve of My Leaving," in earlier forms, from the Artist Book *Painting the Weather*
"My Mother's Garden" and "Winter, American Landscape" in earlier forms, from the Artist Book *The Leap and Fall*
"Limits of Language" *Cordella Magazine, Emergence*

Publisher: Leah Huete de Maines
Editor: Christen Kincaid
Cover Art: "Beeches off the Triangle" by Emily Church 11 x 14" shellac ink on paper 2020
Author Photo: Kate Milford
End Papers: "Marigolds" by Orion Gluckman
Cover Design: Emily Church

Order online: www.finishinglinepress.com
also available on amazon.com

Author inquiries and mail orders:
Finishing Line Press
PO Box 1626
Georgetown, Kentucky 40324
USA

Contents

List of Illustrations

viii   Beech Eyes
6   Beeches in a Sea
11   Watching Forest
18   Beech Roots
22   Maple Arms
28   Climbing Tree

Poems

1   A Million Things to Say
2   Limits of Language
4   Time Traveller
7   Pandemic Summer
9   Summer of Bees
10   Birth Story
12   My Mother's Garden
14   Burden of Love
15   Ginkgo
16   Winter (American Landscape)
19   Lighting the Candles
20   The Cave of Winter
21   To Be A Mother
23   Blue Morning
25   On the Eve of My Leaving
26   Apple Blossoms (Ode to Brooklyn)
29   Swallow
31   Offering
32   Author's Bio

Beech Eyes

A MILLION THINGS TO SAY

There are a million things I want to say
fragments tangled in the corners of my mouth
snared in webs of my hair.
I cannot spit them out.
Things about the haunting look of some trees
and the ache of my children playing simple make believe
in a time when their whole world has been swallowed
and we've spirited away to a land of enchanted forests
mud sucking our boot soles
ceaseless rain
jelly fungi neon yellow oozing from the branches
something new to research under every rock.

Here, a tiger swallowtail with a torn wing
carried home inside the cup of a southern magnolia leaf
nursed on a wedge of orange
taking flight again in the morning
spotted weeks later batting her wings
against the muggy breeze as we traipse again the same trails
citing from our *Golden Nature Guide of Reptiles and Amphibians*
a skink
a box turtle
a ring necked snake
a ribbon garter
a common southern toad speckled in the brown leaf matter.
The weeks blur and radiant green spring deepens
into the heavier scent of summer
and there are a million things to say
beating with whispered wings at the windows
begging to be let out.

LIMITS OF LANGUAGE
for Orion

I see you like the spring opening,
ripe with a fragrance unnameable
a flower we identified incorrectly
attempting to capture your beauty
ultimately indescribable.

Driving the circuitous roads of home
strapped into your throne holding court, you ask
Who invented words? and I am stilled again
your hidden thinking pinning me like a butterfly
set for closer inspection.

A mother should have all the answers, so
casually off the cuff, simple as can be, I say
All our human ancestors made up language,
every word we use to describe the physical world
and also what we cannot see.

Words are not enough.

A name is only letters jumbled together
in order to signify, to identify, to codify
yet, a rose is a rose is a rose,
to name something is to have great power
and I never wanted that responsibility.

Now the name we gave you is set free
untethered from your body, no longer your describer.
It was never truly you, but a placeholder
a title for an idea that someone else (I)
had at your birth.

The reckoning comes suddenly while I am standing
in the middle of the kitchen, dinner plates in hand,
and the name that slips from my lips
seems to arrive with no thought
like it was lying there all the while

beneath the other names
waiting for the days to ripen—
three stars upon your cheek
calling through the universe
to be born again in your body.

TIME TRAVELLER

I am awakened into the day
by the impenetrable light
as it comes to me
glancing through the dirty glass
of my Brooklyn apartment window
warm and orange
as it comes
filtered through the tree,
branches scraping against the beams
splitting the yellow
fracturing space into
cold blue shadows
and the glittering leaves
as they shift in the wind.
The light bounces off my retinas
relays the message of the day,
patterns tapped out to my nervous system
even with eyes closed it penetrates
glowing orange against the lids—

I recall myself to myself—
in the Kentucky dawn,
a child riding along in the backseat
of the tiny four-door sedan
the scent of warmed dust
off-gassing from the upholstery,
small hand pressed against the glass
light pouring in around the shape
the edges of my fingers burning bright
as angels illuminated in the carvings
on the basilica walls at church on Sunday,

my skin iridescent pink
with eyes closed the color is
warm and lush,
the color of blood lit from the outside
lit from a distant star
one in the same with my body
then as now.

Beeches in a Sea

PANDEMIC SUMMER

Cherries ripen quickly
in the June heat wave
from glossy yellow-orange
to a near wine-black
in a matter of days.

We harvest them
standing in the street
beside our car
neighbors suspicious
of our out-of-state plates.

Each night the moon rises
at the appointed hour
over the rooftops across the street
and shines on the waxed floors
of my temporary bedroom.

The street light gleams green
through the thick coverage of leaves
and the moon, a fuzzy ball
in the damp Kentucky air
sits vigil.

The night seethes with sound—
the consuming darkness
cannot swallow the blaring car horns
or the persistent beat of helicopter
propellers, city of unrest.

I sit in paralysis
with a thrumming all around,
vibration, a ticking,
a heat burning off
cooling to a low simmer.

Roses lean bruised heads
against the fence while
bats swoop in chaotic gestures,
memories against the blue night;
a church bell tolls, as from a distant era

announcing the midnight hour
and the lengthening shadows
envelop my body
a shroud, or cocoon, which—
time will tell.

SUMMER OF BEES
for Ursula

The heat wave traps
us together in our
two rooms
moving from one to the
other, seeking to spend
the hours falling, feeding.
You are mute
sometimes smiling.
I try to fill the gaps
with babble
with sensible sound.

Summer of bees and heat
and storms passing over for days.
There is no relief, release.
We are trapped, you and I
passing the hours
in milk
two rooms as one
we are caught in new beginning
neurons forming.

A year before
lazy in my leisure,
I collected glass
among the stones and litter
on a beach in France
as I dreamt of you,
conceived,
bundle of cells
splitting,
smaller than this fragment
azure against my palm.

BIRTH STORY

There was a time when I carried them—
the mothers,
in my car, on my arm, through the tunnels
of subways, to visit the midwife,
through our kitchens, single windowed
and rented, faro and quinoa on the stove
shredding Tuscan kale—
dark greens and grains are good for the milk
when it comes in, hot red and wet
sobbing, we sat on the edges of our tubs
clutching our robes closed over
swollen bodies, bellies shrinking
breasts engorged, enflamed
tender to the touch.
I carried them across an expanse—
entering a pact with them
as we told our birthing stories, about the fear
and the awe, the splitting,
the blood
everything they never tell you in the books
and some things they do.

Watching Forest

MY MOTHER'S GARDEN

In the back corner
beneath the oak leaf hydrangea
I dig up the hip bone
of a long past family dog.
She died in the middle of the night
when I was grown and living elsewhere.
My parents told me about her death rattle
the exhale of her last breath.
I wish they hadn't.
The sound makes me shudder
though I never actually heard it.
I push the bone back into the ground
sick at the thought of finding more,
but curious all the same.
Sifting through the soil
the rest is only fragments
of bone stuck in clay.

The garden is damp and shaded,
a slender strip of sun
along the garage wall
is the only patch of light
in the mess of creeping ivy.
Mosquitoes silently hunt
in the overgrown grass
born out of humidity.
The flowers are thin this summer
after my mother's surgery—
she could not tend them
and so they grow wild and leggy.
The rose bush has a single weary bloom
but when autumn arrives
they will gather against the wall
adding a deep magenta hue
among the shades of green.

I will not return then
to see what becomes
of the limelight hydrangea
planted today in the hole
disrupting the dog's grave
tangled among the roots
carbon feeding the soil.

BURDEN OF LOVE

The weight of your need
lays heavy in the core of me
since my beginning
exhausting with its weary sadness.

Will I misplace this same burden
inside my own children

so that wherever they go
they feel my longing
a cord pulled taught
when they least expect it

as they stand at the kitchen counter
in the morning dawn
waiting for the coffee to brew
dreams receding?

GINKGO

Mom called from Kentucky to say
an old friend has a Ginkgo tree
in her front yard, dropping seeds—
a female.
What a shame! she says,
I feel so bad for her
the fruit smells awful
crushed under foot!

I say, They're beautiful in the fall though.

The berries form a peach flesh mess
on the glass studded paths in the park
across from my apartment
in Brooklyn.
A Chinese family gathers
armed with rubber gloves,
plastic bodega bags over their shoes;
with elaborate pulley-systems
they lasso and bend the branches
of the giant female ginkgo
and shake her free of all her
smelly fruit,
which they collect in nets, like jewels
under golden late fall light.

WINTER (AMERICAN LANDSCAPE)

Walking out among the underbrush
the mistletoe filling in the gaps
Dad is talking about how they plan to clear it all out,
all the things we look for, the odd shapes,
like ribs in the half-light, bones stretched out
over the grass, wrapping around the edges.
The reeds are yellow ochre, but I am thinking
of another color to call them—
something that illuminates, sets them on fire.
He is walking down the paths
made by the park's lawn mower, two lines
between the islands of sleeping trees
and clumps of dead plants—
the invasive species give it character, he says.
He kicks through the grass looking for lost golf balls,
but only clean new ones because he has a bucket full
of rotting ones in the garage.
His dog runs ahead and then back
her straw colored fur blending into the winter field.

A white tree stands limbless in the distance,
a pure trunk stripped of bark and appendages
splitting in two near the top
forming the V of a collarbone,
the whole is a sternum, a Y
a question to the un-answering flat gray sky.
From atop pickle hill
dotted with Van Gogh cypress,
I can see a valley to the left
where the woods begin, and to the right
a road curving through the hills.
Behind, the faint hum of the highway
and through winter black branches,
green exit signs, the big rigs pushing on
through endless American stretches of blacktop.

It is easy to imagine the hills beyond in forest,
populated with the indigenous tribes of Kentucky,
Shawnee and Cherokee among others,
now park names.
Olmsted was here a hundred years ago
urging trees and rocks and plants to form
the shapes we think of as parks.

Dad called the other day to say
the white Y of a tree is gone.
He went looking for it
with his straw colored dog
but it wasn't where we left it
down by the creek.
Only a stump remains
looking ragged and empty.
He counted eighty rings.

Beech Roots

LIGHTING THE CANDLES

Close your eyes to see the echo there
imprinted, a remembrance of the brightness
encountered moments before.
It's called eye color, she said
her baby language suddenly revealed to me
after all this time.
Oh, I say, I see what you mean now,
the memory of the retina replayed on the eyelids.
And which is the true sight?
The one with eyes open?
Or closed?

We stared into the candle flames,
two licking the dark room,
sucking oxygen.
We are made of the same stuff.
Two flames for the first night.
We say the prayer,
nearly getting it right
calling on the light
amidst the dark,
the longest night
in the longest year.

THE CAVE OF WINTER

A hollow chamber of white
snow like static across the screen
the duplicitous reality of perception
white and gray in layers receding
erase what I know is there until I second guess
my knowledge of space and time
of my neighborhood and view from the window.

The cave of winter closes in until I wonder
if we will be here forever inside the flurries
with damp mittens sweating on radiators
snow pants and layers piled like barricades
against the door, while the tea kettle
perpetually comes to a boil
and steam fogs the windows.

The children draw designs of crude snowflakes
the tips of their fingers smudging the glass.
They count the days until birthdays, then spring.
I leap the years instead, the way adults make
five year plans, but I go further than that until
my mind spins a web out and out
encompassing eventually the whole world.

Time suspends inside the falling snow
inside the cave of winter, the sky
a blank page ready to be drawn on
fingers tracing the white, my hand pressed
against the window from behind my glass wall
I try to conjure the world back into being,
to fill in the details of what we cannot see.

TO BE A MOTHER

To be a mother
is to be vulnerable
as the spring opening
every bud exposed
in the balance

waiting for warmth to wake
and fearing the killing frost

that creeps
without warning
in the night after
a long day
of sun
sudden and
unexpected
utterly complete.

Maple Arms

BLUE MORNING

I don't notice the moon anymore
now that I'm not lofted above the city
gazing nightly down
as I've done for the past seven years
like some lonely princess in a tower
except that I'm not alone—
nearly never—
followed around by the plaintive desires of children
even in my private moments.

The needs have followed me here
to the land of thin woods and hollowed trunks.
I can barely make out the upper branches
of the trees that circle me.
I am looking squarely into their lower parts,
root bundles and mid-sections,
all the grooves
and hollows
carved by animal burrowing
and insect toil.
Face to face with the twisting, furry poison ivy vine
thick like my arm
I lean in for a closer look
and it laps at my ankles,
grazes my hips.

These trees block my sky view,
no hint of horizon,
all brown and dull the musk scent of forest
earth and fungi softly sifting under foot
with a backdrop of iridescent green
shimmering spring.

What if I drew them blue,
these mournful trees
my captors
my guardians?
Then would they feel like the infinity
of a New York blue morning?

ON THE EVE OF MY LEAVING

Nostalgia traps
the light, the air
spring
fresh green
scrims across
the landscape
sudden southern thunderstorm
late afternoon
turns the air down, cool lick
everything sparkling
Lucinda Williams on the radio
Sunday country
heart sick for something lost—
nothing tangible
time and place eclipsed
on the slow breezy drive home—
old home, sweet
pints of ice cream forming
condensation crust in the
passenger seat.
Crave, give in
conversation, old friend
where did we go?
lost seventeen, arm out
gliding through this
steaming Kentucky night.

APPLE BLOSSOMS (ODE TO BROOKLYN)

A profusion of bubblegum pink crabapple blossoms
lines the city streets with a cheerfulness
that is nearly obscene
juxtaposed with the landscape
of asphalt and brick
as we speed past in our ubiquitous gray minivan
children caterwauling in the back seats
careening down every possible side street
only to be met with the same endless tail lights—
a typical morning commute.

Is there a poem here
among the garbage swirling
and the daily strain of existing in a space
too crowded with bodies
hurtling toward the day?

At a traffic light
I lament
the lazy
unobservant
incompetent driver
who sat still in the green until it turned yellow
and moved at the last moment
so that now I see red.

Look, say the children:
see those bobbing blossoms over there
see as the morning sun plays upon the pinks
so that they glow like a toxic sunset
see as the wind caresses the tree in slow motion
against the clear impossible blue of sky
shunting down between the bricks
see the chartreuse of newborn leaves just now
before they bloom out and swallow the branches?

Look!
and their innocence pulls me back
into the moment of now, presence of being
wrapped in all my frustrations and joys
like a hot pink blossom, supple and soft
born for today only, bouncing lightly
against the permanence, the sturdiness
of a brick wall.

Climbing Tree

SWALLOW

I walk briskly behind you
as you speed away
on bicycles
dropping them in the dirt
at the foot of a multi-trunked tree
where you hoist yourselves up
defying gravity
skinny arms and legs
scraping the bark
you sit perched above me
two stories up
and crow
at the morning.

I am consumed by you
or is it you by me?
We swallow each other—
merge until we are ouroboros—
I cannot find where I end
somewhere inside of you,
but I remember your beginning,
both of you
ripping into the world
my body split
and now the fact is you
are here, nearly separate
but not quite.

Clinging to my two hands
one for each
sometimes I long for the freedom
to lift my arms
to flick a strand of hair
from my eyes
without your weight
pinning them to my sides

but the pit of you is buried deep—
I feel the tap root curling,
despite my feet on the earth
and yours dangling above me
swinging toward the sky.

OFFERING

Glowing suns
in the palms of your hands
cupped
upturned toward my face
you show me what you've picked
from the transient gardens
the marigolds shine like gems
unfolding and unfurling
tessellating toward the center
the deep pockets
holding secrets
only the bees can know
and you
in your black eyes
recalling other lives, perhaps
when your soul was a ball of light
expanding or contracting
in and again, further in
like the folds of these flowers
you gift to me lightly
though they contain
whole worlds
and you, the explorer
touch them tenderly
as they spill
over the iron fence
faces bent
to kiss the pavement.

Emily Church is a multi-disciplinary artist and curator working in the mediums of painting, drawing, book making, and poetry. Her work takes recognizable experiences—particularly of nature within the urban environment—and transforms them into poetic events. Church grew up in Louisville, Kentucky where the experience of nature coupled with attending an urban arts high school influenced her artistic process. She attended Washington University in St. Louis, earning a Bachelor of Fine Arts in sculpture with a special focus in print and paper making. In 2002, Church studied abroad in Florence, Italy. Since 2008, Church has maintained a studio in the Greenwood Heights neighborhood of Brooklyn. She received a Master of Fine Arts in Painting from the New York Studio School in 2012. Church has attended artist residencies at the Cité Internationale des Arts in Paris, France, the Vermont Studio Center in Johnson, VT, and Yaddo artist colony in Saratoga Springs, NY. Church's paintings and handmade artist books can be found in the collections of The John McEnroe Library at the New York Studio School, The Hyatt Regency of Louisville, KY, Churchill Downs in Louisville, KY the University of Louisville Rare Book Collection, Ekstrom Library, Washington University in St. Louis Rare Book Library, and the Sam Fox School of Art collection, among numerous other private and corporate collections. She lives with her spouse and two children in Brooklyn, NY.

www.ingramcontent.com/pod-product-compliance
Lightning Source LLC
Chambersburg PA
CBHW040307170426
43194CB00022B/2935